EXTREME CAREERS

RACE CAR DRIVERS

Life on the Fast Track

Holly Cefrey

the rosen publishing group's
rosen central

To my family

Published in 2001 by The Rosen Publishing Group, Inc.
29 East 21st Street, New York, NY 10010

Library of Congress Cataloging-in-Publication Data

Cefrey, Holly.
Race car drivers: life on the fast track / by Holly Cefrey. — 1st ed.
p. cm. — (Extreme careers)
Includes bibliographical references (p.   ) and index.
ISBN 0-8239-3367-9 (lib. bdg.)
1. Automobile racing—Vocational guidance—Juvenile literature.
2. Automobile racing drivers—Juvenile literature. [1. Automobile racing drivers. 2. Automobile racing—Vocational guidance. 3. Vocational guidance.] I. Title. II. Series.
GV1029.13 .C44 2001
796.72'023'73—dc21

2001000087

Manufactured in the United States of America

Contents

Start Your Engines

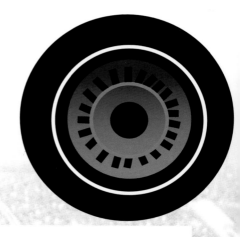

"*I*t was the last five laps of a 500-mile race. I was in second place and I was ready to make a move on the lead car. I'd been closing in on him for the past ten laps, and I was pretty sure that I could catch him before the race ran out.

"My car was running perfectly. The mechanics had spent the entire week building a new engine and working on the suspension. Everything felt smooth and tight as I cruised through the turns, and when I hit the straightaways, my Chevy Monte Carlo lurched ahead as I fed more fuel to the 700-horsepower engine. Everything was a blur but the track in front of me.

"I was in position to challenge the leader. I got right up on his bumper, and waited for a *chance to make a move. I was looking for any little advantage. If he broke the line, or if he let up even a little, I would pull out of the draft and sling right past him.*

"My chance came with two laps left. He gave me just a little room and I went for it. I twitched the wheel to the left and got inside. I could feel the sides of our cars rub as I edged him higher up the bank. We scraped through the corner at 150 miles per hour and he was not backing off. For a second we were both on the edge of being out of control. I kept my speed up and my line tight. Suddenly I broke free. He couldn't hold the corner, and his car fell back to where I could see him in my mirror. I took the checkered flag."
—Ethan Earl, NASCAR driver

Ethan Earl is a professional race car driver who races stock cars. His job is to drive a custom-built car around a specially designed track as fast as he possibly can. Sound like a good job? Ethan thinks so.

"I've always loved driving," Ethan says. "I grew up racing go-karts and eventually I saved up enough money to buy my first stock car." Ethan's first stock

Driving race cars for a living is a job that attracts fiercely independent, competitive thrillseekers.

car was quick, but nowhere near as fast as the Chevy that his sponsor now provides for him. "When I first started racing stock cars," Ethan recalls, "we ran on a dirt track. The fastest we ever went was about 100 miles per hour. It seemed fast at the time." The car that Ethan currently races in NASCAR can reach speeds of 200 miles per hour.

During racing season Ethan and his crew travel to different racetracks around the country and compete in a series of races. At the end of the season his racing record is tallied, and he is given a final score for the entire series. The driver with the most points wins the series championship. Ethan is leading the current series, and is the favorite to win this year.

The Wide World of Racing

The racing world offers a variety of employment opportunities for drivers. There are dozens of styles of racing to choose from. Today's drivers can participate in races that range from oval-track competitions such as the Indianapolis 500 to off-road events like the Safari 2000. Other popular types of racing include Grand Prix, stock car, drag racing, rally racing, hill climbs, sprint car, and go-kart.

Each category of racing is monitored by an association. Associations are groups of people who organize and plan the season-long schedule of races. Associations also create and enforce the rules that drivers must follow if they wish to race.

Grand Prix Racing

Grand Prix racing began way back in 1906. The term "Grand Prix" means "grand prize." It was originally used to describe a country's most important race. Today, the term Grand Prix represents the World Championship of Drivers. The World Championship is a series of races in which the world's best drivers compete.

Automobile races were held as early as 1906.

There are more than fifteen Grand Prix races held throughout the world each year. Germany, Great Britain, Italy, Monaco,

NASCAR races involve stock cars, which look similar to those made by commercial car companies.

and the United States are just a few of the countries that have held Grand Prix races. These races are international events and draw many of the world's best drivers to compete.

The cars of the Grand Prix are raced on city streets or courses that are designed to simulate typical road conditions. Just imagine driving a sports car around your neighborhood at 150 miles per hour, and you'll get an idea of what Grand Prix racing is like. All

Grand Prix cars are single-seater, open-wheel cars that are designed to hug the ground.

Stock Car Racing

Stock car racing began in the 1930s in Daytona Beach, Florida. The major association of stock car racing is the National Association for Stock Car Auto Racing, or NASCAR. NASCAR specifies that the cars raced in the association's series of races must be stock. Stock cars must look very similar to cars made by American automobile manufacturers. In

NASCAR Legend

Robert "Red" Byron is one of NASCAR's all-time top fifty drivers. In fact, he was the first ever NASCAR Points Champion. Before his winning experience with NASCAR, Byron suffered an accident while serving in World War II. Byron was shot down on an air mission. He was unable to walk, and wondered if he would ever race again. After spending several months in military hospitals, he regained the ability to walk. When he rejoined auto racing, he used a steel stirrup bolted onto the clutch to make racing easier for his badly damaged leg. In 1948, after winning eleven races, he was awarded the very first NASCAR championship title.

Drag races are held with cars that reach up to 300 miles per hour on courses usually no longer than a quarter mile.

addition to NASCAR, several other associations organize stock car racing. These include the Automobile Racing Club of America (ARCA) and the American Speed Association (ASA).

Stock cars are usually raced on paved oval tracks. Stock automobiles are of closed-wheel design. Closed-wheel cars have fenders, and the suspension and tires are not exposed as with open-wheel cars. NASCAR checks each car body with templates. Templates are rigid measuring devices placed against an object to make sure that it's designed exactly to the guidelines.

Drag Racing

Drag racing, or hot-rod racing, began in the 1930s. Two drivers race side by side on a one-quarter-mile straight track. The drivers wait for the green light, which signals them to go. When they are given the signal, they hit the gas and don't let up until they pass the finish line. The winner of each race goes on to compete against the next driver until only one unbeaten driver remains.

Drag cars are extremely fast. They can go from 0 to 100 miles per hour in less than a second, and reach speeds of more than 300 miles per hour. What's even more amazing is that they do it on a track only as long as a couple of city blocks. These cars are so fast that they must have parachutes attached to help slow them down after the race.

The National Hot Rod Association (NHRA) and the International Hot Rod Association (IHRA) oversee drag racing events. Drag cars compete in a variety of

A rally drive—like this one in Kenya—is a race of hundreds or thousands of miles over courses unknown to the participants.

classes according to specifications that are set by the sponsoring association.

The fastest of the drag cars include top fuel eliminators and funny cars. Top fuel eliminators have an open-wheel design and use special fuel. Funny cars, with their closed-wheel design, look more similar to the cars we see on the streets every day. In reality, however, they are highly modified machines with thirty times as much power as any car you'll spot driving around town.

Rally Racing

Rally racing began in 1907 when a group of five motorists held a race from Peking to Paris. It was their goal to prove that cars could provide an independent mode of transportation. Luckily for them, they were right, and the winner of the rally drove into Paris sixty days later.

A rally is a race over a public route that the contestants are unfamiliar with. These races can be hundreds or even thousands of miles in length. There are a number of checkpoints along the route. The driver who takes the least amount of time to reach each checkpoint wins the race. In order to locate each checkpoint, drivers take navigators in the car with them.

International rallies are held by the Fédération Internationale de l'Automobile (FIA). Weekend rallies are held locally and regionally across the United States by auto clubs. Rallies have taken place in areas of the world as diverse as East Africa and Australia.

William Hayden is a racer who is competing in this year's Dakar rally. "I feel pretty confident about this year's race," William says. He is sitting in his car making some final adjustments to his custom-built Volkswagen. "This car is incredible," William says as he leans back in the seat. "I can drive this thing over rocks the size of pumpkins and not think twice about it." William's Volkswagen, like all rally cars, has been specially modified to handle ultra-rugged terrain.

William steps out of his car and confides, "I finished slow last year because I didn't have enough power." He pats the hood and smiles, "This year I'm in way better shape. My new mechanic is a genius, and she's done some amazing things to the car. It's never run this well."

William's car is high tech. An intercom system helps the driver and the navigator communicate with each other in the noisy interior of the car. A built-in computer and a sophisticated navigation system will help the team find their way through the shifting dunes of the Sahara Desert.

"Just staying on course is a huge challenge," William explains. "A lot of teams don't even finish the race." William is right. Many drivers find themselves stuck in sand holes, or hopelessly off course. In the worst cases, terrible accidents leave drivers and navigators badly injured.

William estimates that his average speed will be somewhere close to sixty-five miles per hour. If that doesn't impress you, consider this: He will be racing every day for two and one-half weeks over some of the earth's most extreme terrain. Sharp rocks will pound against the bottom of his car and threaten his tires. As he tries to keep his speed up, hundred-foot sand dunes will force him to wind a

Ladies of the Peak

From the first woman who climbed it on foot in 1858 to today's female hill-climb racers, women have always been welcome at Pikes Peak. They have also been successful there, as this list of key dates indicates.

o **1960** Joyce Thompson becomes the first woman to enter the Pikes Peak Hill Climb.
o **1977** Marge Stork is the first woman to finish the race.
o **1984** Michele Mouton becomes the first woman to win a Pikes Peak event.
o **1985** Michele Mouton sets the overall hill record.

twisted course. There are few paved roads in this race. An average car wouldn't last more than a dozen miles.

Hill Climbs

A hill climb is a short-distance race up a winding mountain road. Hill climbing was originally designed as a way to test a car's performance and power. Modern hill-climbing races feature winding curves and rough road surfaces. The driver must race against the clock while challenging the rough terrain of the route. One of the best-known hill climbs in the United States is the Pikes Peak International Hill Climb in Colorado. Every summer since 1916, racers from around the world have brought their cars to this 14,000-foot mountain in hopes of being the fastest driver to the top.

A division of the United States Auto Club (USAC) oversees many hill-climbing events. Many different automobiles can be used in hill climbs, but cars must meet strict safety rules and guidelines in order to race.

A sprint car—distinguishable by the five-foot aluminum wing attached to its top—races at Skagit Speedway in Washington State.

Promoters hope to attract race enthusiasts to indoor kart racing, which is already popular in Europe.

Sprint Car Racing

Sprint car racing started in the early 1900s in the United States on fairground horse tracks. Sprint cars are small racing cars that compete on banked dirt or paved oval tracks. The tracks are usually one-quarter to three-quarters of a mile in length. The Sprint Car Racing Association (SCRA) and the United States Auto Club (USAC) organize sprint events.

A sprint car has the engine in the front and an open-wheel design. Most sprint cars have a roll cage with a five-foot aluminum wing attached to the top. These wings help the cars stick to the track and keep them from sliding too far sideways in the turns.

Karting

Go-kart racing began in the 1950s in the United States. The first kart was made out of unused lawn-mower engine parts. Most kart racing is done on small oval, unpaved tracks. The World Karting Association (WKA) organizes a number of karting events throughout the United States. Major annual karting events take place on speedways such as Daytona International Speedway in Florida.

Karts are basically miniature race cars. They do not have the large amount of horsepower that sprint or stock cars have, but they weigh much less. Their light weight allows them to reach speeds of well over 100 miles per hour.

What It Takes to Become a Driver

"*W*orking on my brother's racing team has taught me a lot. In the beginning, there were just five of us: my brother Frank, my dad, my mom, a friend, and myself. I worked on the car, my brother drove the car, our parents took care of the racing details, and my friend helped me in the pits. It was a real learning experience for all of us. Now Frank races on a nationally sponsored team with hired crewmembers.

"Frank and I raced on the kart circuit for years growing up. We steadily built a reputation as strong drivers. We traveled to the big karting annuals, and did really well there. We had local

companies approach my dad every so often, asking him if we wanted sponsorship. It is pretty common for kart drivers to put a company's sticker on their kart in exchange for free parts. Pretty soon, our karts were plastered with stickers. I loved the kart circuit, but Frank wanted more.

"Frank loved the big cars, and eventually he decided to take the plunge. He was old enough to qualify for the circuit so he started looking into buying a used race car. The cars were pretty expensive, even in used condition, and it seemed crazy to make that kind of investment without even knowing how he would do.

"Then Frank came up with a good idea. He figured if he could get work on the pit crew of an established driver, he might have a chance to see what driving the big cars was like. He asked around and located a driver who needed a crewmember. My brother worked for him, and pretty soon the driver agreed to let him take a few practice laps in the car.

"My brother knew that he wanted to race stock cars after the very first practice. He also

It is a good idea for aspiring race car drivers to get the feel of the racing environment by working on the pit crew of an established driver.

knew that he would have to quit his job to pursue a full-time racing career. Quitting his job meant that he would give up a regular paycheck. Basically, he would have to go to work for himself. He talked our parents into helping him get sponsors so that he could try to get his own car and get started on his career.

"Our parents hadn't negotiated on that level before . . . the sponsorship of a car can cost tens of thousands of dollars, easily. It was a good thing that my family already had a strong racing reputation. It helped get sponsors to listen to my parents. They eventually found two sponsors: a local restaurant chain and an automobile dealership. The dealership helped us work out a way to lease a race car that would normally cost $100,000.

"My brother learned quickly that to make sponsors happy, you have to win. The first years, or rookie years, can be very tough and hard fought. Not only are you competing as a driver, but as an underdog, too. The track is a lesson in itself. My brother usually did well enough to qualify, but the races were tough, and *there were a lot of experienced drivers with huge sponsors and great cars.*

"Then Frank had one amazing season, which changed everything. He took first place in three features. It was so cool hearing his name echo over the stands as he took his victory lap. Before we knew it, my parents were getting calls about national sponsorship. After a ton of negotiating, my brother picked up a national sponsor. Along with the sponsorship came a real pit crew, and my brother was given a small salary. I was hired onto the crew, and was also given a small starting salary. My brother is incredibly happy to have reached his goal, and my parents are proud to say that we have a professional racer in the family."
  —*Marisa, twenty-three years old*

Frank and Marisa's experience in racing is a fortunate one. Not all new drivers are able to overcome all of the challenges and find a way to win. New drivers quickly learn that there is more to racing than just driving fast. There is also the business side of racing. Drivers have to find sponsors and keep them happy. In any form of racing, drivers need perseverance. They have to have the desire to

Starting small—driving in local or regional races—is the way to hone your driving skills so that you can work your way up to bigger races.

race as well as the desire to invest money—or find funding—to support their racing careers.

Building Your Career

The investment you make in your driving career is not only about money; it's also about time. Some drivers prefer to race part-time, on an amateur level, while other drivers strive to make racing their sole source of

A driver's income comes from winning races, sponsorships, product endorsements, and public appearances.

income. Racers do not usually commit to full-time professional racing until they are sure that they can afford it, and that there is a good possibility of success.

Many racers try to gain a good deal of racing experience before making a full-time commitment and getting into the more expensive types of racing. By starting small, you can gain experience and grow as a driver without the added pressures of worrying about money, sponsorship, or winning. Starting small will allow you the freedom to experiment with different racing styles at your own pace.

As Frank's story illustrates, a racer essentially works for himself or herself. You are in charge of building your own career, which can remain on an amateur level or become a full-time profession. As amateurs, most racers have other jobs that help to pay for car parts and repair costs as well as everyday living expenses.

Sponsorship Perks

Average starting salaries for professional racers start moderate to small. An estimated base salary for a typical racer in the United States is $20,000. The

Aside from driving, a racer also needs to be able to communicate well with the crew about the car's performance, even in the middle of a race.

starting salary of a professional racer is determined by the driver's past racing experience, individual sponsors, and team racing funds.

Amateur and professional racers are also given cash prizes for winnings. The winnings vary for each form of racing and each circuit or series. Aside from sponsorships, earnings can come from product endorsements and public appearances. Some sponsors also award year-end bonuses if the season was successful.

What It Takes to Make It

Besides the time and finances, there are individual qualities that a driver must possess in order to experience success. Drivers need to possess the desire to learn. A formal education is not required to be a race car driver—amateur or professional—but drivers will benefit from a strong knowledge of the rules and regulations of their sport, and of their racing association's policies.

Drivers also need to understand the machine that they are racing. They need to be able to handle it with skill and ease. Racing is a fast-paced, highly unpredictable sport. Many skilled but nonetheless rookie drivers can add to the probability of accidents or unpredictable events on a track. Drivers need nerves of steel and strong instincts in order to handle any unforeseen events.

Driver Duties

Besides knowing how to drive well, drivers have other job duties. Drivers have to communicate effectively to the crew about the performance of the car.

Race Car Drivers: Life on the Fast Track

This communication takes place during downtime, test runs, practice laps, and even during the races themselves. Drivers must also have an understanding of racing equipment and supplies in case the mechanic is unavailable to assist.

Successful drivers have a strong sense of sportsperson-like conduct. They behave in ways on and off the track that reflect a healthy racing style and attitude. Professional drivers are required to make public appearances to support the team and the sponsor's image. Drivers are also expected to strictly follow an association's rules, as well as attend all mandatory driver meetings.

Life as a Race Car Driver

Racing is an extreme sport. Drivers compete with each other in a sport that demands both technical knowledge and physical strength. But knowledge and stamina by themselves are not enough to win. Successful race car drivers must possess one other quality: nerves of steel.

Every step in a race car driver's life presents new challenges. Whether a driver is a rookie on a local level or a seasoned Winston Cup winner, he or she will encounter new challenges at every turn. Drivers who choose to meet these challenges head-on and are determined to overcome any obstacle that stands in their way, will be rewarded with victory.

Amateur racers who wish to become professionals have to find ways to balance the stresses of real-world

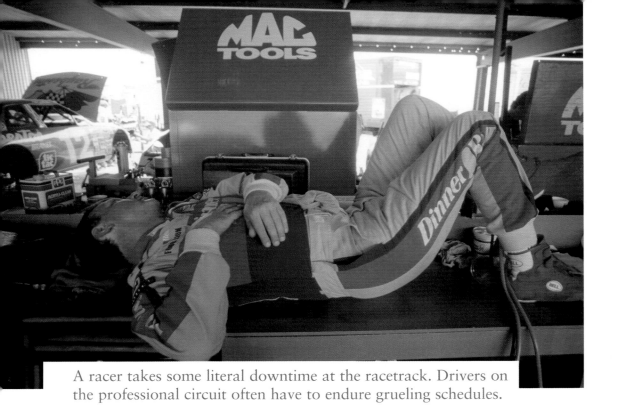

A racer takes some literal downtime at the racetrack. Drivers on the professional circuit often have to endure grueling schedules.

work or school while preparing for the weekend's races. Racers who have broken into the professional ranks have challenges of their own to meet. They struggle to find quality downtime while meeting the demands of a grueling schedule.

"I'm basically living out of a suitcase. I joined the stock car team as a rookie after doing well in the truck racing series. I am finishing my

season in the truck series and building towards my Winston career. I have a schedule like you wouldn't believe.

"Sometimes I sleep in the trailer. Other times, when the schedule permits, I stay at a hotel. When I get to the hotel I try to relax, but I find myself thinking about my upcoming crammed schedule. It's a tough one, but if the season goes well, it'll be worth the work. Here's this season's schedule:

September 17th—Winston Cup test in Charlotte, North Carolina

September 18th—Craftsman Truck test in Delaware

September 19th–20th—Craftsman Truck races in Delaware

September 20th–22nd—Winston Cup races in Delaware

September 27th–30th—Winston Cup races in Virginia

October 1st–2nd—Winston Cup test in Georgia

October 3rd–7th—Winston Cup races in Charlotte

October 9th–10th—Winston Cup test in Rockingham, North Carolina

October 11th–13th—Craftsman Truck races in Texas

October 16th–17th—Winston Cup test in Arizona

October 19th–21st—Winston Cup races in Rockingham

October 23rd–24th—Winston Cup test in Florida

Race Car Drivers: Life on the Fast Track

October 25th–26th—Craftsman Truck races in California
November 3rd—Craftsman Truck banquet in Arizona

"If the season goes well, I will be scheduled to do public appearances all over the country. Many big-time racers have public appearances scheduled during a tight racing season. That's a challenge— keeping track of a racing career while working on a public image. It's a twenty-four-hour job. The traveling, racing, practicing, and meet-and-greets increase as you build your career. I have a lot to look forward to, and a lot to learn."

—Sandra, twenty-two years old

Staying in Racing Shape

Along with mental demands, race car driving presents physical challenges. As the cars are driven around turns or a track, gravitational forces work against the racer's body. The racer's muscles are tensed or flexed to work against the gravitational push against the body. As many races last over an hour, this can put quite a strain on the body.

Many racers practice some sort of exercise regime to ensure that they are up to the demands of racing. Many racers also do cardiovascular exercises, which strengthen the heart muscles and aid in circulation. It's also wise to follow a healthy, energy-boosting diet. Long hours at the track before and after races can be very energy-depleting. Eating the right foods can ensure that a racer is giving his or her body the best chance of facing the challenges of racing.

The Risks of Racing

Above and beyond the thrills and challenges of racing, there are also risks.

In a split second, a racer's life can change for the worse. There are no second chances on the track. One wrong move or unforeseen event can send a racer and his or her car crashing into a wall or into another car.

A driver relies on a harness, which is like a heavy-duty seat belt, to keep him or her safe during a crash. Many improvements have been made on belts and harnesses, but driver safety is never guaranteed. Even

While it is an exciting sport and career choice, racing cars is also a field where a split second can mean the difference between life and death.

when the belt works—and keeps the driver in his or her seat during a crash—the sheer force of the body pressing against the belt at 150 miles per hour can cause injury.

"I would have been racing this weekend. I would have been with my family and friends at the league race. Instead, I am at the Alexandria hospital recovering from a crash that changed my life. I've been in a few other accidents, resulting in a broken bone or two. That's the life of a racer, we all know it. This crash was different, though. I keep thinking about what I could've done to avoid it.

"My car slammed backwards into a wall at 180 miles per hour. I was unconscious when the paramedics got to me. My car was totaled, and I was crushed in between bent metal. The paramedics had to free me carefully from the wreck. I underwent emergency surgery and awoke in the hospital a few days later.

"This is the first week that I have been out of my hospital bed. I have a motorized wheelchair that allows me to move around. I am going

Wreck Museum

The International Motorsports Hall of Fame displays the remains of race cars that have been totaled in accidents. These exhibits are designed to illustrate how safety features have improved over the years. The wrecked autos belong to driver Phil Parson, from the Talladega wreck in 1983, and driver Michael Waltrip, from the Bristol wreck in 1990.

through some very intensive workouts, trying to get the ability to walk again and to get sensation back in my legs. A month ago I was worried about how many races I would win this year. Now I worry about what I'm going to do with the rest of my life if I can't race again.

"Last season was incredible. I won my first national. The thought of my success is bittersweet now. It

happened to me at a time when racing was all that there was for me. I would have made any sacrifice to race, as most racers would. The thrill of racing is awesome. Meeting every challenge to win is what racing is about. When you don't win, you rack up lessons for the next one. When you wreck, you either walk away from it . . . or you don't. I am determined to get back on the track, but it is going to take a lot of hard work."
   —Junior, twenty-six years old

Getting Up to Speed

*"**I** became interested in racing on the day that my friends and I went to the local kart ranch. The karts only had three horsepower engines, but there was something so fun about racing against the other karts. I talked to a lot attendant who told me about the sprint car races that take place on the outskirts of the city. My mom and I went to the weekend race and sat in the grandstands.*

"The smell of fuel and the sound of the motors sent a chill through me. They had all kinds of classes that raced that night. Races started with younger kids and finished with adults. After the races we were allowed to enter the pits. I spoke with one of the winners while

officials were inspecting his car. He was in the adult races, but he was only fifteen. I told him that I was interested in becoming a racer and he told me about racing school. He attended a racing school, which he felt was helping him to get ahead as a racer. He gave me a brochure about the school.

"The brochure was really informative. It presented information about safety, racing equipment, what was expected of the students, and the cost of attending classes. I convinced my mom to let me attend the summer intensive program. My mother said that she would match a dollar for every dollar I saved towards the cost of attending. I raked leaves, babysat, cleaned the garage, did housework, and any other odd job I could find to earn money for school.

"I attended the summer intensive and learned how to race. The instructors taught us how to drive carefully while also being competitive. I learned about the cars, and how to become a racer. I also learned how to budget expenses for a hobby like racing. The following year, I joined the association and raced as a

rookie in the junior class. I was able to race because of what I learned in school. Without the school, I would have had to learn everything on my own, and probably through costly mistakes. I placed second in the point standings at the end of the year, and was given a huge trophy."

—Lou, thirteen years old

Foot Work

If you are interested in a particular form of racing, learn all that you can about it. Visit local race shops that sell engine parts or racing gear. Employees will most likely know of races or tracks in your area. By calling local racetracks you can find out if your kind of racing is done there. Track representatives should be able to tell you where your races might be occurring—if not locally, then regionally. If possible, ask a parent to help you attend a race to get a good look at what it's really like.

Another great source that can help you to locate races that occur locally and regionally is the Web. Using the resources at the back of this book, you can contact associations that organize many types of races. Many national associations have smaller divisions or local chapters that can help you to locate races.

After locating a local race and finding out if it's of real interest to you, try to speak with one of the racers, preferably when he or she is not busy with racing details. Ask if it's okay to observe the process close up, but try to stay out of the way. The pits are as fast and furious as the track.

School Search

There are over 100 racing schools or programs in North America. Several schools specialize in only one form of racing, such as Formula One, stock car, or karting. Some schools also provide in-depth training for other careers in racing. A few colleges offer degrees for careers in the world of racing. A degree can allow a person to start off in a better position and with a better salary than a person with no training or education. Also, if driving doesn't work out, you'll have a degree in the field that you can rely on for another career option.

Drivers can gain valuable experience and credentials at any
of the 100 racing schools throughout the United States.

As with any educational program, it's important to thoroughly research race schools that you are considering attending. You can also ask to speak with graduates or past students of the school or program. They will be able to give you honest answers about the value of the school or program.

Questions to Consider

Here is a list of questions to consider when looking into a school or program. A school or program representative should be able to provide answers that will give you an idea of the experience provided by that institution.

◆ How much is the overall cost of the program, including mandatory supplies, or costs beyond tuition?

◆ What are the minimum requirements to attend the school or program?

◆ Have you had serious injuries or fatalities at your school?

Race Car Drivers: Life on the Fast Track

◆ What equipment am I required to bring?

◆ What physical condition do I need to be in to take this program?

◆ Do I need to pass a physical before applying?

◆ Is the program a racing or a driving program? (You're looking for racing, although many schools offer both.)

◆ Are there scholarships and financial aid available for the school or program?

◆ Do top graduates of the program get special funding to join a racing series or an award of any kind?

◆ Does graduating from the program qualify me for the type of racing I'm interested in?

◆ How much time is actually spent racing or on the track?

◆ Do I drive my own car, or is the car shared with other drivers?

◆ How fast will I be going?

◆ Are there students at your school of my age or gender?

◆ What makes your school better than other schools?

British racing legend and instructor Jim Russell gives a student a few pointers.

Start Your Engine !

No matter which style of racing you are interested in, there are a number of career paths that you can follow to reach your goal as a professional racer. The key to getting your career started is to get involved with racing. Whether you decide to work for a racing team at the local racetrack or enroll in a driving program, you are educating yourself about the sport of racing. This first-hand experience will help you in deciding which type of racing you want to pursue.

Glossary

CART (Championship Auto Racing Teams) An association that organizes open-wheel Indy car races and sports car racing.

chassis The metal structure underneath the body of a car that the rest of the car is built around.

closed-wheel Refers to cars that have fenders and tires which are therefore not exposed. Stock cars, sports cars, trucks, and touring cars have closed wheels.

crew chief The coach of a race team who is responsible for overseeing pit stops as well as the development of the driver.

drag race A race from a standing start on a flat, straight surface.

Formula One A type of racing that uses open-wheel cars. Formula One race courses are commonly laid out on city streets.

Race Car Drivers: Life on the Fast Track

funny car   A type of closed-wheel drag racing car that can reach speeds of more than 250 miles per hour.

IHRA (International Hot Rod Association)   An association that oversees many types of drag racing.

Indy car   An open-wheel, open-cockpit car traditionally raced at the Indianapolis 500.

kart   A miniature open-wheel automobile specifically designed for racing.

NASCAR   (National Association for Stock Car Auto Racing)   An association that sanctions about 2,000 races annually.

NHRA (National Hot Rod Association)   An association that sanctions several categories of drag races.

open-wheel   Refers to cars that have their wheels, tires, and suspension exposed. Indy cars and Formula One cars are open-wheel cars.

pit   An area located on the inside of a racetrack where drivers have their cars serviced and repaired before and during a race.

pit crew   The team of people who services a race car.

pit stop   When a driver stops his or her car for service during a race.

pole position   The best position in which to start a race, in the front row on the inside lane.

qualify   When a racer is allowed to enter a race based on the results of test sessions.

sponsor   A company that pays a racing team to carry its name.

stock   Any car or part made by an automobile manufacturer that has not been modified.

top fuel   The fastest type of drag racing cars. These cars have an open-wheel design.

Winston Cup   NASCAR's top race series, which began in 1949.

For More Information

In the United States

Automobile Racing Club of America (ARCA)
P.O. Box 5217
Toledo, OH 43611-0217
(734) 847-6726
Web site: http://www.arcaracing.com

The International Hot Rod Association (IHRA)
9 1/2 East Main Street
National City Bank Building, 2nd Floor
Norwalk, OH 44857
(419) 663-6666
Web site: http://www.ihra.com

**National Association for Stock Car Auto
 Racing** (NASCAR)
P.O. Box 2875
Daytona Beach, FL 32120
(904) 253-0611
Web site: http://www.nascar.com

National Hot Rod Association (NHRA)
2035 Financial Way
Glendora, CA 91741
(626) 914-4761
Web site: http://www.nhra.com

Professional Sports Car Racing
14175 Icot Boulevard, Suite 300
Clearwater, FL 33760
(727) 533-0503
Web site: http://www.professionalsportscar.com

The Sprint Car Racing Association (SCRA)
P.O. Box 50937
Phoenix, AZ 85076
(562) 804-1718 (hotline)
(480) 940-2354 (office)
Web site: http://scra.com

World Karting Association
6051 Victory Lane
Concord, NC 28027
(704) 455-1606
Web site: http://www.worldkarting.com

In Canada

Canadian Association for Stock Car Auto Racing
  (CASCAR)
9763 Glendon Drive
Komoka, ON N0L 1R0
(519) 641-1214
Web site: http://www.cascar.ca

Racing News and Information on the Web

CBS Sportsline—Auto Racing
http://www.sportsline.com/u/racing/auto

Crash.net
http://www.crash.net

ESPN.com—Motor Sports
http://www.espn.go.com/auto

National Kart News
http://www.nkn.com

North American Motorsports
http://www.na-motorsports.com

WhoWon.com—Motorsports News
http://www.whowon.com

Racing Schools on the Web
Check out these Web sites, schools, or programs on the Web to learn more about educational opportunities for racers:

Autosport Basi Racing School (Canada—open-wheel racing)
http://www.autosportbasi.com

Bridgestone/Firestone Racing Academy (Canada)
http://www.racef2000.com

Complete Auto Racing School (C.A.R.S.) (California—stock cars and trucks)
http://www.carsracing.com

Competitive Edge (Idaho, Oregon, and Washington stock cars)
http://www.racingschool.com/imecorp/compedge.shtml

Drive to Victory Lane (Connecticut)
http://www.drivetovictorylane.com

FinishLine Racing School (Florida)
http://www.finishlineracing.com

Jim Russell Racing Drivers School (California)
http://www.russellracing.com

RaceKarts Inc. (California—karts, drivers ages eight and up)
http://www.racekartsinc.com

RacingJobs.com
http://www.racingjobs.com

RacingSchools.com (online source for racing schools)
http://www.racingschools.com

Richard Petty Driving Experience
http://www.1800bepetty.com

Team O'Neil Car Control Center
http://www.team-oneil.com

Touring Car Club (California)
http://www.touringcarclub.com

For Further Reading

Huff, Richard M. *The Making of a Race Car.*
Philadelphia: Chelsea House, 1998.

Savage, Jeff. *Racing Cars.* Mankato, MN: Capstone
Press, 1996.

Smith, Jay H. *Kart Racing.* Mankato, MN: Capstone
Press, 1995.

Stewart, Mark. *Auto Racing: A History of Fast Cars and
Fearless Drivers.* New York: Franklin Watts, 1999.

Sullivan, George. *Burnin' Rubber: Behind the Scenes
in Stock Car Racing.* Brookfield, CT: Millbrook
Press, 1998.

Wukovits, John F. *The Composite Guide to Auto
Racing (Composite Guide Series).* Philadelphia:
Chelsea House, 1999.

Index

About the Author

Holly Cefrey is a freelance writer and researcher. She was raised in a racing family. In their spare time, all members of her immediate family have worked in the world of racing. Her brother has raced as a World Karting Association member and a stock car racer, her father has worked as a tech official and mechanic, and her mother has worked as a scoring official.

Photo Credits

Design and Layout

Les Kanturek